# A Dickens of a Christmas

First published 2015

Text copyright © Richard Cole

All rights reserved. No part of this publication may be reproduced, stored in or introduced into a retrieval system, or transmitted, in any form or by any means (electronic, mechanical, photocopying, recording or otherwise), without the prior written permission of the publisher. Any person who does any unauthorized act in relation to this publication may be liable to criminal prosecution and civil claims for damages.

**There are no performing rights required or any fees to be paid for any amateur production of this work.**

This book is sold subject to the condition that it shall not, by way of trade or otherwise, be lent, resold, hired out, or otherwise circulated without the publisher's prior consent in any form of binding or cover other than that in which it is published and without a similar condition including this condition being imposed on the subsequent purchaser.

## A DICKENS OF A CHRISTMAS

Cast:

Mrs Dickens – very proud of her famous husband
Scrooge – a mean skinflint
Bob Cratchit – Scrooge's long suffering clerk
Fagin – leader of the pickpocket gang
Oliver – a kind boy who has got in with a bad crowd
Artful Dodger – a pickpocket and likeable rogue
Nancy – a kind lady who tries to help Oliver
Ghost of Christmas past

Ghost of Christmas present
Ghost of Christmas future
Mr Pickwick – a jolly old soul who is very loud and boisterous
Mrs Pickwick – his outrageous partner!
Tiny Tim – a poorly child who gets our sympathies
Little Dorrit – another suffering child
Victorian people (one person with a bag of hats!)

# A DICKENS OF A CHRISTMAS

**"OUR HOUSE" by Madness is playing as the scene opens with some children running in and knocking on Scrooge's door. They run off and hide before he appears. This is repeated, as the song is acted/danced/sung.**

**TINY TIM (on crutches?) and LITTLE DORRIT are among the crowd of street urchins.
Enter MRS DICKENS**

MRS DICKENS: Oh it's you pesky urchins again. Driving poor Mr Scrooge mad with all your silly games. Haven't you got homes to go to?

**The children look very sad as they shake their heads.**

|  | Oh no I forgot – you are all orphans with no homes. |
|---|---|
| TINY TIM: | Some of us have got home, like little Dorrit and I. |
| LITTLE DORRIT: | But you can't call Tiny Tim's place a comfortable home. No thanks to Mr miserable Ebenezer Scrooge! |

**SCROOGE sticks his head out of the door**

| SCROOGE: | Someone talking about me again? |
|---|---|
| TINY TIM: | Good morning, Mr Scrooge. How nice to see you. |
| SCROOGE: | Nice to see me? Nice to see me? Why? Just because I pay your father so much money that he can spoil you children with luxuries? Get away from my house! |

**SCROOGE goes back in, shouting:**

|  | Cratchit? Get me a coffee. Now! |
|---|---|
| MRS DICKENS: | Here we go again! Shouting in the street and my husband Charles Dickens, the author, is trying to work upstairs. **(She calls up to her** |

husband) Are you still writing your novels, Charles?

**Three taps are heard on the floor.**

Oh good, he's still alive! Trouble is, I never see him. He just gets so involved with his writing that he spends days and nights slaving away over a hot pen.

TINY TIM: Really? Do you mean he just writes and writes and never comes out to see you?

MRS DICKENS: That's about it. One day he will write a famous book and we will become rich and famous.

LITTLE DORRIT: How can you be sure?

MRS DICKENS: I just know that Charles Dickens will become a famous author. I have Great Expectations!

TINY TIM: Great Expectations would be a good name for a book too!

LITTLE DORRIT: Great idea. Will you tell your husband?

MRS DICKENS: Definitely. He gets all of his ideas from just observing people. **(She shouts up to Charles).** I said you get all your ideas from observing people. **(Three knocks reply).** Little Dorrit here says that Great expectations

|  |  |
|---|---|
|  | would be a good title for a book. **(Three knocks).** |
| TINY TIM: | What about using Mr Scrooge as a subject for a book. |
| LITTLE DORRIT: | That would be a good idea. |
| MRS DICKENS: | It won't be a good idea if he overhears you! |
| TINY TIM: | I don't care! |

**The three characters move forward and are unaware that SCROOGE comes out of his house while they are talking! The OTHER CHILDREN shrink back.**

|  |  |
|---|---|
| LITTLE DORRIT: | He gives me the creeps! |
| MRS DICKENS: | And me. He is a really awful man. |
| TINY TIM: | I hate the way he keeps saying humbug about everything. |
| LITTLE DORRIT: | And he is so mean with his money! |
| MRS DICKENS: | Your father, who works for him, never seems to complain. If I were he I'd be asking for a pay rise. |
| TINY TIM: | Who agrees that my Dad should get a pay rise? |

**All respond (encourage audience)**

LITTLE DORRIT: Who thinks Mr Scrooge is a terrible skinflint?

**All respond (encourage audience)**

| | |
|---|---|
| SCROOGE: | Humbug!! |
| MRS DICKENS: | Ooh…Mr Scrooge. We didn't hear you creeping up on us. |
| TINY TIM: | Have you been there for a long time? |
| LITTLE DORRIT: | I am sorry. I didn't mean to call you a terrible skinflint. |
| SCROOGE: | For your information, miss, I am not a terrible skinflint. I am an *excellent* skinflint. And as for Tiny Tim's father getting a pay rise….? You have read my thoughts – it was just what I was thinking of doing. |
| MRS DICKENS: | Oh, Mr Scrooge – thank you – we take it all back what we said about you. |
| TINY TIM: | Were you really thinking of giving my father more money? |
| SCROOGE: | Yes. I was thinking about it. But now, after your outburst, I am thinking…..NO! |
| MRS DICKENS: | Ebenezer Scrooge – you will never change. |
| SCROOGE: | Oh yes I will. |
| **ALL:** | Oh no, you won't! |
| SCROOGE: | Oh yes I will. |
| **ALL:** | Oh no, you won't! |
| SCROOGE: | I will. I will. I will! |
| **ALL:** | You won't! You won't! You won't! |
| SCROOGE: | OK. I won't! No pay rise for your father. And all I can say to you miserable shower |

(**pointing at audience**) is something very sweet.

ALL: Something sweet?

SCROOGE: HUMBUG!

**SCROOGE stomps back indoors as the VICTORIAN enters, as a postman. The OTHER CHILDREN leave.**

MRS DICKENS: Well I hope my husband Charles Dickens, the author, makes old Scrooge into a memorable character in one of his books.

TINY TIM: Me too.

LITTLE DORRIT: Me three.

VICTORIAN: Excuse me. I have a parcel here for a Mr Bob Cratchit.

TINY TIM: That is my father. May I take it?

VICTORIAN: Well it has to be signed for.

LITTLE DORRIT: Well Tiny Tim can sign for it, surely.

VICTORIAN: My name's not Shirley!

**Whole cast do high fives to celebrate the return of the old joke!**

MRS DICKENS: So where is the parcel from?

VICTORIAN: Probably from Amazon.

**There is an awkward pause as they all look at each other. They move forward to discuss the problem.**

MRS DICKENS: I think we are trying to establish a Victorian flavour this year.

| | |
|---|---|
| TINY TIM: | My history is pretty poor but I don't think Amazon.. |
| **ALL:** | Other booksellers are available. |
| TINY TIM: | I don't think that Amazon would have been in existence in Victorian times. |
| LITTLE DORRIT: | Can you change the line to something really old – something Victorian? |
| VICTORIAN: | OK. Something really old. **(He points at audience member).** It came from them! |
| MRS DICKENS: | Amazing! |
| VICTORIAN: | Sign here please. And make sure that your Dad gets it forthwith. |

**He moves back once it is signed for, continuing to check his post.**

| | |
|---|---|
| TINY TIM: | A parcel for father! He never gets parcels. What ever can it be? |
| LITTLE DORRIT: | Hadn't you better take it to him? |
| MRS DICKENS: | I can't think Mr Scrooge is going to take kindly to your father receiving parcels during work hours. |
| TINY TIM: | That's true. What would you suggest? |
| LITTLE DORRIT: | Why not just leave it on the doorstep for him to pick up when he comes out. |
| MRS DICKENS: | **(pointedly)** What a great idea. And nothing could ever happen to it, surely! |

**VICTORIAN enters quickly**

VICTORIAN: My name's not…
MRS DICKENS: We've done the Shirley joke already!

**VICTORIAN exits, saying sorry.**

TINY TIM: OK. I will leave the parcel on the doorstep. It should be absolutely fine.
LITTLE DORRIT: I have a great idea.
MRS DICKENS: What is it?
LITTLE DORRIT: It's like a thought or a vague notion.
MRS DICKENS: Thanks. I know what an idea is – but what is *your* idea?
LITTLE DORRIT: We could get the audience to keep an eye on it.
TINY TIM: Brilliant!
MRS DICKENS: And so original in a show!

**The parcel is placed in a prominent place.**

MRS DICKENS: Do you think the audience can be trusted?
TINY TIM: Hmmm. Not sure. What could we do to find out?
LITTLE DORRIT: I have another idea.
MRS DICKENS: What is it?

| | |
|---|---|
| LITTLE DORRIT: | It's like a thought or vague notion. |
| MRS DICKENS: | **(losing it)** I KNOW WHAT AN IDEA IS! You already told me. |
| TINY TIM: | Sorry Dorrit – what do you think we should do? |
| LITTLE DORRIT: | Let's test the audience. |
| MRS DICKENS: | One original idea after another this year! |
| TINY TIM: | I will go out and come back in. If you see me near the parcel you must shout out… |
| LITTLE DORRIT: | Snowballs! |
| MRS DICKENS: | Snowballs? Why snowballs? |
| TINY TIM: | Why not? It's nearly Christmas. |
| LITTLE DORRIT: | Clever link! |
| MRS DICKENS: | Will you do that for us? |

**Audience respond**

| | |
|---|---|
| TINY TIM: | They don't sound too sure! |
| LITTLE DORRIT: | Will you do that for us? |

**Better response hopefully. MRS DICKENS and LITTLE DORRIT go off in one direction. TINY TIM circles round the stage and then goes near the parcel.**

| | |
|---|---|
| **AUDIENCE:** | Snowballs! |

**MRS DICKENS and LITTLE DORRIT slowly come in.**

MRS DICKENS: Did they shout, Tim?
TINY TIM: Yes, Mrs Dickens!
MRS DICKENS: Well I couldn't hear anything. Try again.

**Sequence is repeated with better response. They run back in this time.**

MRS DICKENS: Brilliant – so much better. Now you two must go and we must let the show continue.

**TINY TIM and LITTLE DORRIT leave.**

MRS DICKENS: On with the show. Ladies and gentlemen, in honour of my husband, Charles Dickens, the author, we present "A Dickens of a Christmas!"

**SET PIECE: The stage fills with chickens. (Shake your tail feathers, there ain't nobody here but us chickens etc.) . It finishes and MRS DICKENS comes back in, shouting:**

MRS DICKENS: I said "Dickens" not chickens!

**The chickens start to leave, making their apologies! SCROOGE comes out and shoos them all away. BOB CRATCHIT, who follows him like a little dog, joins him. He is clearly scared of SCROOGE.**

**The VICTORIAN (dressed as sandwich seller) also appears.**

| | |
|---|---|
| SCROOGE: | What on earth is going on now? Chickens? Get moving! I only like poultry in motion! Come on, Cratchit…do something useful for once in your miserable life. Get rid of these chickens. |
| BOB CRATCHIT: | Yes, Mr Scrooge. Whatever you say, Mr Scrooge. Now come on, you chickens, would you mind moving along there please? Thank you so much. |
| SCROOGE: | Don't be nice to them! Show them who's boss! Move it you feather brain! |

**CRATCHIT starts to leave as well!**

| | |
|---|---|
| SCROOGE: | Not you, Cratchit! Give me strength! |
| VITORIAN: | Would you like a nice sandwich, Mr Scrooge? |
| SCROOGE: | What sort? |
| VICTORIAN: | The kind that's made with bread. |
| SCROOGE: | Ha ha very funny. Have you got any meat sandwiches? |
| BOB CRATCHIT: | Mr Scrooge is rather partial to a rasher of bacon. |
| VICTORIAN: | Sorry, gents. No meat today because the butcher had a bit of a mishap. |
| SCROOGE: | What sort of mishap? |

VICTORIAN: He backed into the bacon slicer and got a little behind in his orders!

BOB CRATCHIT: I don't suppose I could have a cheese sandwich, could I?

SCROOGE: Who said you could join in this shopping extravaganza? No!

BOB CRATCHIT: Sorry, Mr Scrooge, I just thought…

SCROOGE: Well that is where you went wrong. You are not paid to think!

BOB CRATCHIT: (**aside**) I'm not paid much for anything!

SCROOGE: What's that you are saying, Cratchit?

BOB CRATCHIT: Nothing Mr Scrooge.

SCROOGE: You're mad if you are talking about nothing. I shall dock your pay accordingly for wasting business time. Now, sandwich seller (who looks remarkably like the postman but no one seems to have noticed that), what is your cheapest sandwich?

VICTORIAN: It all depends on the filling, sir.

SCROOGE: OK. So what is your cheapest filling?

VICTORIAN: A sandwich with nothing in it!

SCROOGE: Perfect. I'll have one of those then!

VICTORIAN: What? Just two pieces of bread?

SCROOGE: Don't be ridiculous; this is for my clerk, Bob Cratchit. Do you honestly think I would buy him two pieces of bread?

VICTORIAN:         Sorry, sir. My mistake.

SCROOGE:           It is your mistake. I will have one piece of bread, folded!

**The VICTORIAN gives him the bread and leaves, disgusted.**

SCROOGE:           Here you are, Cratchit. One cheese sandwich.

BOB CRATCHIT:      Thank you, Mr Scrooge. But there is no cheese in it!

SCROOGE:           Moan, moan, and moan! For goodness sake, Cratchit, put a sock in it!

BOB CRATCHIT:      Sorry, sir.

SCROOGE:           You imbecile! If you want a cheese sandwich you can have one. (**He reaches in his pocket**)

BOB CRATCHIT:      Thank you very much.

SCROOGE (**offering old sock**): This cheesy enough for you? Mange tout! And for pudding….

BOB CRATCHIT:      Pudding?

SCROOGE:           HUMBUG!

**SCROOGE goes back indoors.**

BOB CRATCHIT:      What am I to do? Mr Scrooge is so cruel to me sometimes. But I am very grateful as well because, with the little money he gives me, I can at least provide for my dear family.

**He spots the parcel on the side but does not go too near (in case the audience start shouting out!!)**

BOB CRATCHIT: Oh look! A parcel…and it's for me. What can it be?

**Enter MRS DICKENS**

MRS DICKENS: Bob Cratchit! You've got a parcel! Oh, I see you've found it!

BOB CRATCHIT: Hello Mrs Dickens. How exciting is this? A parcel – whatever can it be?

MRS DICKENS: Well pick it up and find out – open it up!

**SCROOGE sticks his head out of the house**

SCROOGE: Cratchit! Stop wasting time and get me another coffee!

**SCROOGE goes back in and BOB CRATCHIT trots after him, leaving the parcel where it is.**

MRS DICKENS: That poor Mr Cratchit. And all he wants to do is open his parcel. Mr Scrooge is horrible to him. My husband, Charles Dickens, the author, really should put him into one of his stories. **(She calls to her husband).** Mr Dickens, are you still writing your novels?

**Three taps are heard.**

MRS DICKENS: Good. Keep going – and make sure that you make Mr Scrooge into a nasty old skinflint. **(Back to audience).** Though I think old Scrooge has already made himself into a nasty old man. Mind you, from what I hear, he has been having bad dreams recently and has started sleepwalking. Do you know what that is? When people are in a deep sleep they suddenly get up and start walking around in a daze. You'll probably see it happen in the audience if this script doesn't improve soon! **(There is a noise off – it is the PICKWICK's making their entrance!)**
Uh oh…I think no one will sleep if that is who I think it is. Watch out – here come Mr and Mrs Pickwick! I'm off!

**She leaves.**

**The PICKWICKS are a very colourful, loud pair. They enter from different points and eventually meet and greet in the centre.**

PICKWICK: Well helloooo there all you gorgeous souls!

| | |
|---|---|
| MRS PICKWICK: | What have we here? My, what a simply splendid selection of social misfits. (**To audience member**) Look at that lovely outfit – is it a designer label? Oxfam shop was it? |
| PICKWICK: | Look at that person there – with the body of a super-model. |
| MRS PICKWICK: | More like a supermarket if you ask me! |

**They meet in the centre and do an over the top welcome/dance which involves a lot of bumping into each other and falling about.**

| | |
|---|---|
| PICKWICK: | As I live and breathe it's the beautiful Mrs Pickwick, light of my life and leading fashion guru. Give us a twirl! (**She does**) |
| MRS PICKWICK: | Mr Pickwick, Mr Pickwick, Mr Pickwick – how lovely to bump into you in this run down area! All this misery and suffering. They really should get a decent scriptwriter! |
| PICKWICK: | You look wonderful, sweet pea. How do you manage to come up with such a cornucopia of clothes to dazzle and delight? |
| MRS PICKWICK: | I get dressed in the dark. |
| PICKWICK: | But just look at this audience – don't they look wonderful? |
| MRS PICKWICK: | They really are awesome. |
| PICKWICK: | Possibly a mixture of wonderful and awesome… |

| | |
|---|---|
| MRS PICKWICK: | You mean…? |
| PICKWICK: | Fulsome and awful!! |
| MRS PICKWICK: | Let me tell you about a strange thing that just happened to me. |
| PICKWICK: | Someone in the audience laughed at a joke? |
| MRS PICKWICK: | I said it was "strange" not a "miracle"! Yes, I was in that lovely pudding and pie shop when a penguin wandered in and sat down to eat! |
| PICKWICK: | A penguin in the pudding and pie shop? |
| MRS PICKWICK: | The penguin in the pudding and pie shop picked a pumpkin pie. |
| PICKWICK: | Pardon? |
| MRS PICKWICK: | You heard! |
| PICKWICK: | So, the penguin in the pudding and pie shop picked a pumpkin pie. What is strange about that? |
| MRS PICKWICK: | Penguins eat fish. |

**The joke should fall very flat!**

| | |
|---|---|
| PICKWICK: | That seemed a huge amount of alliteration and a smattering of onomatopoeia for a weak ending. |
| MRS PICKWICK: | I said it was strange not funny! |
| PICKWICK: | Oh, Mrs Pickwick, you are the funniest lady alive! |

MRS PICKWICK: If I've told you once, I've told you a million times – don't exaggerate!

**They spot the parcel.**

PICKWICK: Ooh look, a parcel. I wonder whom it can be for?
MRS PICKWICK: Well, we could go and take a look.
PICKWICK: That should be fine – no harm in that.
MRS PICKWICK: No harm at all. We will just go over to the parcel and no one will know we have been near it.
PICKWICK: Exactly. It's not as if the audience are going to shout out "snowballs" if we go near it, is it!

**They go near and the audience shout out. MRS DICKENS rushes in.**

MRS DICKENS: What are you doing near Bob Cratchit's parcel?
MRS PICKWICK: We were just taking a quick peep! No harm in that is there?
PICKWICK: Well Bo did it…

**The ladies stop and stare at him**

| | |
|---|---|
| MRS DICKENS: | What? |
| MRS PICKWICK: | Have you had too many wine gums again Mr Pickwick? |
| MRS DICKENS: | What do you mean, "Bo did it"? |
| PICKWICK: | Peeped…Bo peeped! |
| MRS DICKENS: | Sheepish looks everywhere please! |
| MRS PICKWICK: | Oh, Mr Pickwick, what a wonderful wit you are! |
| MRS DICKENS: | Something like that! |

**SCROOGE, followed by BOB CRATCHIT, enters. SCROOGE is sleepwalking!**

| | |
|---|---|
| SCROOGE: | Sheep – sheep – where have the sheep gone? |
| BOB CRATCHIT: | Mr Scrooge! You are sleepwalking again! |

**They all follow SCROOGE as he roams around.**

| | |
|---|---|
| PICKWICK: | Oh my word – whatever next? |
| MRS DICKENS: | I heard that old Scrooge was having strange dreams. But sleepwalking?! And in broad daylight too! |
| MRS PICKWICK: | What do we do? |
| MRS DICKENS: | Don't wake him up – that's for sure. Let's watch what happens. |

| | |
|---|---|
| SCROOGE: | Look at all the lovely sheep – **(the names are bleated)** Baaarbara, Baarclay, Shaun, Ewan and Tony. |
| BOB CRATCHIT: | Tony? A sheep called Tony? |
| PICKWICK: | Probably Tony Blaaair! |
| MRS DICKENS: | This is fun! I must tell my husband… |
| ALL: | Charles Dickens, the author. |
| MRS DICKENS: | Oh good, you've heard of him! |
| SCROOGE: | Get away from me! I don't want ghosts near here! |
| BOB CRATCHIT: | Ghosts? Did he say ghosts? |

**The CAST freeze in fear (apart from SCROOGE). By this time, the THREE GHOSTS have appeared. Only SCROOGE can see them.**

| | |
|---|---|
| SCROOGE: | I can see you. Who are you? You keep coming to me in my dreams. What do you want? |
| GHOST of PAST: | I am the ghost of Christmas Past |
| | Shedding truth on things that last. |
| | Greed and poverty – side by side |
| | Scrooge's past is opened wide. |
| GHOST of PRESENT: | And I, the ghost of Christmas present, |
| | Should be able to see things pleasant |
| | But look at what your greed has done |
| | Yet it could change before rise of sun |
| GHOST of FUTURE: | Then in my turn I too shall tell |

|  |  |
|---|---|
|  | The future, but it does not look well |
|  | Ebenezer Scrooge will suffer more |
|  | Each time he steps out through his door. |
| SCROOGE: | What do you mean? I will suffer? I don't want to suffer! |
| GHOST of PAST: | Too late, too late to change what's past |
| GHOST of PRESENT: | The present woes are here to last. |
| GHOST of FUTURE: | The future, Scrooge, you still could fix |
|  | But not until you see our mix. |
| SCROOGE: | Mix? What mix? |
| GHOST of PAST: | The past. |
| GHOST of PRESENT: | The present. |
| GHOST of FUTURE: | The future. |
| ALL THREE GHOSTS: | The mix…the mix…the mix… |

**The GHOSTS of PRESENT and FUTURE leave as they say the last line. Their voices fade away and the CAST come out of their trance. SCROOGE stands staring into the space where the ghosts once stood. The GHOST of PAST follows SCROOGE like a shadow.**

|  |  |
|---|---|
| MRS DICKENS: | What shall we do? |
| PICKWICK: | Perhaps we should leave? |
| MRS PICKWICK: | A good idea. He gives me the creeps under normal circumstances let alone when he is sleepwalking! |
| BOB CRATCHIT: | I'd better stay with him. |

| | |
|---|---|
| MRS DICKENS: | Bob Cratchit, you are a marvel. Anyone else would walk away from that old goat – especially the way he treats you. |
| PICKWICK: | Well done, Cratchit. I'm sure he will appreciate you one day. |
| MRS PICKWICK: | Don't hold your breath! A leopard can't change its spots. |
| BOB CRATCHIT: | I'll be fine. Just leave and we'll see what happens. |

**The others leave. SCROOGE wakes up. Although the GHOST is there, the characters do not see it.**

| | |
|---|---|
| SCROOGE: | Cratchit! Why are you not working? |
| BOB CRATCHIT: | Oh thank goodness, Mr Scrooge – you've woken up. |
| SCROOGE: | What are you whining on about? |
| BOB CRATCHIT: | You've been sleepwalking, sir. |
| SCROOGE: | Oh no – not again. I keep getting these recurring nightmares but this is the first time that I have had a day mare! |
| GHOST of PAST: | Scrooge? Ebenezer Scrooge? |
| BOB CRATCHIT: | Well he's gone now, Mr Scrooge. |
| SCROOGE: | You mean you can't hear the voices? |
| GHOST of PAST: | Scrooge? Ebenezer Scrooge? |
| SCROOGE: | Get away from me, spirit! Leave me alone! |

**SCROOGE runs away from the GHOST. CRATCHIT cannot see the GHOST so does not know what is happening.**

BOB CRATCHIT: I'm concerned, Mr Scrooge. I am going to get a doctor. You stay here. Don't go away. Promise.

SCROOGE: A doctor, yes, that's it… a doctor. Perhaps I need a doctor. But don't go spending loads of money on him – get the cheapest you can!

**BOB CRATCHIT runs out, leaving SCROOGE with the GHOST of the PAST**

GHOST/PAST: So, Ebenezer, it is just you and I now. Are you ready to see where it all went wrong for you?

SCROOGE: Yes, spirit…show me. Please. Show me.

**Enter a group of happy CHILDREN, playing tag etc. One (the young Scrooge) does not join in but is reading. The GHOST points out various things to SCROOGE as they happen.**

GHOST/PAST: Can you see yourself there, Ebenezer?

SCROOGE: Yes. That's me – the one not joining in the games.

GHOST/PAST: And why, Ebenezer? Why did you not join in?

SCROOGE: I thought I should study to get a good job. That's why I am reading instead of playing.

GHOST/PAST: And watch what happens – you had chance after chance.

**The children try to encourage young Scrooge to join in but he refuses. One girl even blows him a kiss. But young Scrooge refuses to join in. The CHILDREN leave and young Scrooge looks sadly after them.**

| | |
|---|---|
| SCROOGE: | I had chances but let them go. But I had to get a good job and earn plenty of money. |
| GHOST/PAST: | And how was that achieved? |
| SCROOGE: | Workhouses. A great idea – it gave children a roof over their head and good meals. Didn't it? |
| GHOST/PAST: | Watch, Ebenezer. Watch. |

**The second SET PIECE takes place – a Victorian workhouse: "Food, glorious food", pickpockets etc. FAGIN, DODGER and OLIVER merge into the scene as it ends. They are lurking in the scene as the next part develops. OLIVER is sat in full view, watching proceedings. FAGIN and DODGER are less obvious to the audience.**

| | |
|---|---|
| SCROOGE: | I had no idea. I thought the workhouses would be a good idea. |
| GHOST/PAST: | But you never went to check, did you? |
| SCROOGE: | No. I didn't. |
| GHOST/PAST: | And now we have more theft on the street than ever before. Your fault, Ebenezer. You drove people into poverty and crime. **(the GHOST leaves, saying)** Your fault, Ebenezer. Your fault. Your fault. |
| SCROOGE: | GO AWAY! |

**BOB CRATCHIT and the VICTORIAN (now a doctor) rush in.**

VICTORIAN: Mr Scrooge. It's Doctor Marigold. Are you OK?

SCROOGE: It was terrible doctor. I was with a ghost in the past. I saw my miserable upbringing and those dreadful workhouses.

VICTORIAN: Perhaps you should come to my surgery.

BOB CRATCHIT: Oh please go, Mr Scrooge. I will look after the business while you are away.

SCROOGE: Perhaps I should. Thank you, doctor. You have a kind face – not dissimilar to the postman and sandwich seller!

VICTORIAN: It's the cutbacks, sir.

BOB CRATCHIT: Oh, I thought it was a coalition!

SCROOGE: Cratchit – go and tend to the business. Doctor – take me to the surgery.

VICTORIAN: Walk this way.

**The VICTORIAN does a "strange" walk off which the others mimic.**

**After a few moments, NANCY appears, looking for OLIVER and the others.**

NANCY **(calling softly at first)**: Oliver?.... Oliver?... Where are you?

**OLIVER sneaks up behind NANCY as she searches for him. The audience will help her find him.**

NANCY: Oh no. I can't find Oliver anywhere. I do hope he hasn't got involved with that Mr Fagin and his gang of thieves.. Now where could he be? Can anyone see him?

**"Behind you" business with audience and eventually OLIVER is discovered**

OLIVER: Nancy! Were you looking for me?
NANCY: You know I was! What have you been up to?
OLIVER: Well, I was told to come into town and wait for instructions.
NANCY: Instructions? Instructions from whom?

**DODGER jumps out.**

DODGER: That's for me to know and you to find out!
NANCY: Dodger! That's all we need. And if the Artful Dodger is here that no doubt means that Fagin will be close by…

FAGIN (stepping out of the shadows): Nancy. Oliver. Dodger. My dears..how lovely to see you again. And what is this I hear you saying about Mr Fagin and his gang of thieves? Are you suggesting that I would associate with such lowlifes?

**DODGER and FAGIN are now stood close to one another.**

DODGER: What us? Associate with lowlifes and thieves? Never.

FAGIN: Just look around….can you see any such people?

**FAGIN and DODGER spot the audience and recoil in horror!**

DODGER: Cor! Strike a light. How did that dodgy lot get in?

NANCY: You can't say that to the audience!

OLIVER: Why do you think they are dodgy, Mr Fagin?

FAGIN: Dodgy, Oliver? Dodgy? There's only one person on this earth that deserves the title of "dodgy".

DODGER (bowing): At your service, laddies and jellybabies!

NANCY: No wonder they call him the Artful Dodger!

| | |
|---|---|
| OLIVER: | But why are we here in town? You told me to come and wait for you. Are we going to play some games? |
| FAGIN: | Games. Yes…games. |
| DODGER: | I can't do games. I've got a note from my mum! |
| FAGIN: | Dodger! You 'aint got a note and you 'aint got a mum neither! |
| DODGER **(overacting like mad)**: | Oooh that hurts. Fancy reminding me that I am an orphan… no mother **(sob)**…. No father **(sob)**….no family **(sob)**… no place to call home **(sob)**….. and I will tell you somethin' else too…. |
| ALL: | What? |
| DODGER: | No games neither! |
| NANCY: | Oh, Dodger, that breaks my heart. Give me a hug! |

**NANCY stretches out her arms for a hug. DODGER likes this idea and turns his back on her for a moment to smarten himself up. FAGIN steps in between NANCY and DODGER. DODGER turns round to hug NANCY and ends up hugging FAGIN!**

| | |
|---|---|
| DODGER: | Oh Nancy! |
| FAGIN: | Oh Dodger! |
| DODGER: | Oh crikey! |

**DODGER and FAGIN split and try to recover from their embarrassment. FAGIN tends to keep on the move, looking around in case the law are approaching.**

| | |
|---|---|
| NANCY: | Now that was funny! |
| OLIVER: | But I still don't know why we are here. |
| FAGIN: | Well, Oliver, it's like this. The people that live in these streets are what we call "posh". They have houses and fine clothes and other riches. |
| DODGER: | Some might say they have too much riches and wealth. |
| NANCY: | And I suppose you want to relieve them of some of those riches! |
| OLIVER: | Relieve them of their riches? Whatever do you mean? |
| FAGIN: | Redistribute the wealth around the poor. That is….me! |
| DODGER: | And me! |
| FAGIN: | Of course, Dodger. I meant "us" of course. |
| DODGER: | That would be a first! |
| NANCY: | You mean stealing! |
| OLIVER: | Stealing! |
| FAGIN: | Sssh! Don't use such coarse language – it is not fitting of a lady or a well brung up boy. I hate the word stealing. |
| DODGER: | He hates the word but he loves the actual stealing! |

NANCY: What about getting caught though?

FAGIN: That is where the skill comes in.

DODGER: He never gets caught!

NANCY: Don't be too sure, Fagin.

OLIVER: But how do you do this stealing, Mr Fagin?

FAGIN: Would you like a demonstration of the fine art of nicking, purloining and lifting valuables form others without any detection?

DODGER: Or would you like to see us nick something and not get caught?

NANCY: I think stealing is wrong and you shouldn't be encouraging Oliver to get involved.

OLIVER: Thank you Nancy. You are very sweet to look after me.

FAGIN: **(mocking)** "Thank you Nancy. You are very sweet to look after me."

DODGER: **(mocking)** "Thank you Nancy. You are very sweet to look after me."

**They both pretend to be sick!**

NANCY: That's right – mock us. Just because we want to live honest lives.

FAGIN: Honest lives? Honest lives? How can we live honest lives when people like Scrooge are

|  |  |
|---|---|
|  | ripping people off and amassing stacks of money whilst we have to beg and steal? |
| DODGER: | Hear hear! Those toffs have everything they need and more. |
| NANCY: | It does seem unfair. |
| FAGIN: | That Ebenezer Scrooge spends a fortune on coffee each day! |
| DODGER: | Instead of treating his workers properly and giving them a good wage he drinks away all the profit. He's coffee crazy! |
| NANCY: | But stealing won't make things better, will it? |
| FAGIN: | It will make things better for me! |
| DODGER: | Me too! |
| NANCY: | Well I'm having nothing to do with it. Crime does not pay! Come on, Oliver. |

**She leaves.**

|  |  |
|---|---|
| OLIVER: | Goodbye Mr Fagin. Goodbye Dodger. I hope to see you again soon. |

**OLIVER starts to leave but is pulled back**

|  |  |
|---|---|
| FAGIN: | Oh what a shame. Just when Dodger and I were going to play a game. |
| DODGER: | I can't do games, I've got a note! |

**FAGIN knocks DODGER's hat off!**

FAGIN: I said, Dodger, we were going to play "a game"!

DODGER: Oh…."a game"…sorry Fagin…I didn't realise it was a "game".

OLIVER: What game? Perhaps I could play.

FAGIN: Of course, Oliver. This game is called "pick a parcel".

DODGER: It's a great game. Everyone should play it.

OLIVER: But how do we play it?

FAGIN: You see that parcel over there, Oliver? **(Pointing to CRATCHIT's parcel)** I wonder if one of us could get it without the audience shouting out "snowballs"?

DODGER: Worth a try. Let's see if we can distract the audience!

**During this next part, FAGIN and DODGER are sneaking towards the parcel. If the audience do call out "snowballs" they move away and tell them to shush!**

FAGIN: Labels and gentle spoons, boils and curls. Perhaps you would like to go for a stroll.

DODGER: They're not moving, Fagin!

FAGIN: Free chocolate in the car park!

DODGER: Still not budging!

| | |
|---|---|
| FAGIN (**suddenly pointing to the roof**): | Look! |
| DODGER: | Father Christmas! |
| FAGIN: | This show is going to go on forever at this rate! |
| DODGER: | What do you mean? It already has gone on forever! |
| FAGIN: | Those seats are really uncomfortable. What Charles Dickens would call "Hard Times"! Why not have a wriggle? |
| DODGER: | Not a wriggle in sight **(points to one person)** Apart from them – they've been wriggling all the time. |
| FAGIN: | Probably got ants in their pants! |
| DODGER: | Come on, wriggle! Wriggle, wriggle, wriggle! |

**FAGIN and DODGER do a "wriggle" dance as they repeat the last line. During this they suddenly make a grab for the parcel and throw it back and forth. The audience shout "Snowballs", MRS DICKENS, NANCY, the VICTORIAN(now a policeman) TINY TIM and LITTLE DORRIT rush in and, in the confusion, OLIVER catches the parcel. All freeze with OLIVER in the centre.**

| | |
|---|---|
| MRS DICKENS: | Someone's taken the parcel. Thanks, audience! |
| FAGIN: | Well look at that! He's stolen a parcel. |
| DODGER: | What is the world coming to? |
| TINY TIM: | But that parcel is for my father! |
| LITTLE DORRIT: | Fortunately there is a postman… |

**The VICTORIAN coughs and shakes his head.**

I mean a sandwich seller…

**The VICTORIAN coughs and shakes his head.**

A doctor then?

**The VICTORIAN coughs and shakes his head.**

Then what are you this time?

| | |
|---|---|
| VICTORIAN: | Hello, hello, hello. What's going on here then? |
| ALL: | Oh, you're a policeman! |
| VICTORIAN: | Did anyone see what happened? |
| TINY TIM: | That boy has got my father's parcel! |
| LITTLE DORRIT: | He's a common thief! |
| MRS DICKENS: | Whatever next? The world is in a mess – it's all of a twist! All of a twist? **(calling up)** Mr Dickens! Write down "all of a twist" as a possible book title! |
| VICTORIAN: | I think you're going to have to accompany me to the police station. |
| TINY TIM: | Why? |
| VICTORIAN: | I get scared if I go on my own. |
| TINY TIM: | What if he was to put the parcel back? |
| LITTLE DORRIT: | Could we not let him off? |

| | |
|---|---|
| MRS DICKENS: | Let him off? That makes him sound like a firework! |
| VICTORIAN: | The law is the law. If I apprehend a villain in the street then it is my duty to escort them to the cells. |
| OLIVER: | If I must. I'm sorry to have caused so much trouble. |

**SCROOGE emerges from his house. The GHOST of PRESENT unobtrusively joins the crowd.**

| | |
|---|---|
| SCROOGE: | Now what's going on? All this noise outside my house – quite put me off my coffee. Move along, you ruffians,. |
| VICTORIAN: | Sorry to trouble you, sir. I'll soon have this sorted out. |
| FAGIN: | Dodger, do you have anything to say? |
| DODGER: | Scarper! |

**Exit FAGIN and DODGER.**

| | |
|---|---|
| VICTORIAN: | Move along then, everyone. There's nothing to see. |

**They all leave apart from SCROOGE and the GHOST of the PRESENT.**

| | |
|---|---|
| GHOST/PRESENT: | Are you happy about that? |
| SCROOGE: | No. I am not. My coffee is getting cold. Cratchit will have to make me a fresh cup |
| GHOST/PRESENT: | Is that all you care about? |
| SCROOGE: | Why not? If I don't look after myself then who is going to? |
| GHOST/PRESENT: | Hardly the Christmas spirit! |
| SCROOGE: | Christmas! Bah! Humbug! |
| GHOST/PRESENT: | But you have created the Christmas rush! |
| SCROOGE: | What are you talking about? And who are you? |
| GHOST/PRESENT: | I am the ghost of Christmas present. |
| SCROOGE: | I hate Christmas presents – what a waste of money! |
| GHOST/PRESENT: | And yet you do very well out of it, Ebenezer. |
| SCROOGE: | Absolutely. I increase my charges, make sure that the shops only get their supplies from me and then I sit back and listen to the cash tills ringing! |
| GHOST/PRESENT: | Is that what you see? What about the real meaning of Christmas? |
| SCROOGE: | Bah! Humbug! |
| GHOST/PRESENT: | Is it? Let's see! |

**SET PIECE: there is an eruption of Christmas shoppers all arguing and having a real hassle in the sales. Appropriate music blasts out (Slade? It's Christmas!) In amongst it there are carol**

**singers and, perhaps, a nativity scene. The frantic shoppers ruin these**

| | |
|---|---|
| SCROOGE: | That is not my fault. |
| GHOST/PRESENT: | Not yours entirely. |
| SCROOGE: | Thank you. |
| GHOST/PRESENT: | There are other selfish people too. |
| SCROOGE: | Selfish? Me? Selfish? |
| GHOST/PRESENT: | Yes, Ebenezer Scrooge. And people hate selfish people. They hate you. Hate you. Hate you. |

**The GHOST of Christmas PRESENT leaves, repeating the line.**

| | |
|---|---|
| SCROOGE: | Stuff and nonsense! **(He calls out)** CRATCHIT? Bob Cratchit! Come here immediately. |

**Enter BOB CRATCHIT**

| | |
|---|---|
| BOB CRATCHIT: | Sorry, Mr Scrooge. I was so busy working… |
| SCROOGE: | Good. Now tell me, Cratchit. Am I selfish? |
| BOB CRATCHIT: | You Mr Scrooge? |
| SCROOGE: | Yes me, imbecile! There's no one else here apart from … |

**(SCROOGE looks around for the GHOST and is concerned to see no one there)**

BOB CRATCHIT: Are you looking for someone, sir?

SCROOGE: Am I alone here, Cratchit?

BOB CRATCHIT: Well, I'm here Mr Scrooge.

SCROOGE: Idiot! I know you are here! But what about the answer to my question. Am I selfish? Am I popular? Do people like me?

BOB CRATCHIT: Well…

SCROOGE: Yes?

BOB CRATCHIT: Well…

SCROOGE: Well what?

BOB CRATCHIT: Well, *I* have never called you selfish, sir.

SCROOGE: Exactly. I knew I was right. Now stop loitering in the street, go and get some work done and make me a fresh coffee!

BOB CRATCHIT: Yes, Mr Scrooge.

**CRATCHIT goes back indoors.**

SCROOGE: All this rubbish about me being selfish. And as for all that Christmas nonsense….bah! Humbug!

**Enter MRS DICKENS, TINY TIM and LITTLE DORRIT. They bring back the parcel and hand it to SCROOGE**

| | |
|---|---|
| TINY TIM: | We got the parcel back. Shall I give it to my father? |
| SCROOGE: | No. He's too busy working. |
| LITTLE DORRIT: | And making you coffee, no doubt! |
| SCROOGE: | But of course! I have to have a coffee to keep my mind alert. |
| MRS DICKENS: | Just how much coffee do you drink each day? |
| SCROOGE: | All of it! What a stupid question! |
| TINY TIM: | I think Mrs Dickens was wondering how much you spend on coffee as well! |
| SCROOGE: | And what business is that of yours? Anymore impertinent questions and your father will be out of a job! Now put his stupid parcel back over there and leave me in peace. |

**The parcel is put back on view.**

| | |
|---|---|
| LITTLE DORRIT: | We didn't mean to upset you Mr Scrooge. Especially so close to Christmas Day. |
| MRS DICKENS: | Oh, of course! It's nearly Christmas! |
| SCROOGE: | Christmas? Bah! Humbug! |
| TINY TIM: | Why are you so mean to everyone? |
| LITTLE DORRIT: | Can't you see all the hardship and suffering out here? |
| SCROOGE: | What, the audience? |
| TINY TIM: | No! The people who have no money and cannot enjoy Christmas. |

| | |
|---|---|
| LITTLE DORRIT: | Could you not give them some paid work? |
| MRS DICKENS: | What a good idea. Go on, Mr Scrooge, break the habit of a lifetime and give us some work. |
| SCROOGE: | Well all right. I suppose you could all clear the ice off the pavements in front of my shop. |
| TINY TIM: | That's more like it! Thank you. |
| LITTLE DORRIT: | I didn't think you cared for the customers at your shop. I was wrong. |
| MRS DICKENS: | Very thoughtful of you to care about people's safety. |
| SCROOGE: | I don't give a monkey's about their safety. If they fall over then they can't spend money in my shop! |
| TINY TIM: | Typical! |
| LITTLE DORRIT: | Would you mind if we stood outside your house and sang Christmas carols? |
| SCROOGE: | You can stand in the middle of the street and caterwaul to your heart's content. With any luck a horse and cart will plough you down. Christmas carols? Bah! Humbug! |

**SCROOGE stomps back indoors.**

| | |
|---|---|
| TINY TIM: | What *is* his problem? |
| LITTLE DORRIT: | Too much coffee. |
| MRS DICKENS: | Too much money. |

| | |
|---|---|
| TINY TIM: | Too few friends. |
| LITTLE DORRIT: | Poor man. |
| MRS DICKENS: | Hardly "poor". He makes an absolute fortune each Christmas and keeps it all for himself. What a skinflint! Selfish old toad! |
| TINY TIM: | Considering my father pays him rent each week you'd think he would do something about improving our home. |
| LITTLE DORRIT: | No wonder you are always ill, Tim. Your house is in a terrible state. |
| MRS DICKENS: | Leaking roof, mouldy walls and the damp is rising so fast the mice are wearing life jackets! |
| TINY TIM: | It's still my home though. And it's a house full of caring people. My family love me and I love them. |
| LITTLE DORRIT: | And someone has sent your father a parcel. Any idea what it might be? |
| MRS DICKENS: | My curiosity is killing me! Let's open it. (**to audience**) No need to shout "snowballs" this time. Hope you are keeping up with the plot! |
| TINY TIM: | Come on then – let's see what it is. |

**They sneak across to the house and get the parcel. They open it furtively and reveal the charity collecting boxes**

| | |
|---|---|
| LITTLE DORRIT: | Charity boxes? Why would your Dad want them? |

**There is a noise from off stage (the PICKWICKS are approaching)**

MRS DICKENS: Oh lawks! There's someone coming! Hide the parcel – they might think we are stealing it!

**The parcel is passed from one to another during the next sequence.**
**Enter the PICKWICKS**

PICKWICK: Well here we are again – just when you thought you could sleep!

MRS PICKWICK: Oh, Mr Pickwick, what jolly japes the audience have been experiencing in our absence.

PICKWICK: You can see on their faces just how much they have missed us.

MRS PICKWICK: So, what has been going on?

**Probably no response!**

PICKWICK: My, you have been paying attention.
MRS PICKWICK: Perhaps we could have a recap?
PICKWICK: What a wonderful notion, my dear.
MRS PICKWICK: A recap! A recap!
PICKWICK: But who can do the recap?

MRS PICKWICK: It would have to be someone who has been here all along!

**They scan the audience as the VICTORIAN enters, carrying a basket (full of hats and props)**

PICKWICK: Ah, a passing Victorian who should know what has been going on. Unlike the audience!
MRS PICKWICK: Come on, young man. Tell us what has been happening.

**They all sit down to watch. The VICTORIAN recaps the story, using each hat in turn.**
VICTORIAN: This is the story of Dickens (not chickens) and miserable old Scrooge. The postman delivered a parcel for Bob Cratchit and the audience had to shout out "snowballs" if anyone went near it. We saw how mean Scrooge was when he put a smelly sock in a sandwich he bought from a terrifically handsome sandwich seller **(pose)**. A few ghosts came and spooked out Mr Scrooge("woohooo") and showed him how poor the people had become. Another stunningly good-looking doctor **(pose)** appeared before Fagin and his gang tried to take the parcel. That gorgeous policeman **(pose)** made a popular entrance before we saw how awfully selfish people had become at

Christmas. Then the Pickwicks came in and asked me what was happening. And that's about it.

**He rushes off! The CAST all applaud and call him back.**

PICKWICK: Wonderful! But I'm not sure I understood it all.
MRS PICKWICK: Could you possibly tell us again?
VICTORIAN: But that would take ages!
PICKWICK: Well do it quickly then!
MRS PICKWICK: As fast as you can!

**The VICTORIAN now gabbles through the story, using the hats and props accordingly!**

VICTORIAN: Dickens – chickens – postman **(pose)** – parcel – snowballs – sandwich **(pose)** – poor people - ghosts – doctor **(pose)** – Fagin – theft – policeman **(pose)** that's about it!

**The VICTORIAN collapses in a heap!**

PICKWICK: He's collapsed! Fetch a policeman!
MRS PICKWICK: He *is* the policeman!
PICKWICK: I had no idea! What a wonderful piece of acting!
MRS PICKWICK: But what happens next?
TINY TIM: And what shall we do with these collecting boxes?

| | |
|---|---|
| LITTLE DORRIT: | Mr Scrooge won't be happy to find charity boxes near him! |

**SCROOGE comes out of the house with BOB CRATCHIT. The parcel is with TINY TIM**

| | |
|---|---|
| SCROOGE: | What is going on? |
| BOB CRATCHIT: | It's my son, sir. And he seems to have my parcel! Tim? What is going on? |
| MRS DICKENS: | We just *had* to know what was in your parcel. |
| TINY TIM: | That's right, father. I am sorry. |
| LITTLE DORRIT: | We all wanted to know – not just Tim. |
| SCROOGE: | So what is this great mystery, eh? |
| MRS DICKENS: | Oh, it's nothing, Mr Scrooge! |
| SCROOGE: | It seems much ado about nothing. |
| MRS DICKENS: | Now that would be a good title for my husband, Charles Dickens |
| ALL: | ..the author! |
| TINY TIM: | Too late I fear – William Shakespeare already used it! |
| SCROOGE: | Hurry up and tell me or you will be like William Shakespeare – you'll all be barred! |
| LITTLE DORRIT: | Perhaps we should show him. |
| MRS DICKENS: | OK. On your head be it. |

**TINY TIM reveals the charity boxes**

SCROOGE: What is all the fuss about? It's only two boxes!

TINY TIM: Charity boxes, sir.

SCROOGE (**clutching his chest**): Charity? CHARITY! Take it away! Take it away! (**SCROOGE collapses**)

LITTLE DORRIT: Oh no! We've killed him!

MRS DICKENS: Fetch the doctor, quickly!

**They all shout for the doctor. The Victorian rushes in (as a policeman!)**

VICTORIAN: Hello, hello, hello…

ALL: Doctor! Doctor!

VICTORIAN: oops…my mistake. This is the hardest part ever!

**The VICTORIAN rummages through the hats and finds the doctor's eventually! As this distraction is happening, the GHOST of the FUTURE has entered and stands watching.**

VICTORIAN: Stand back. Give me room.

**The CAST step back (apart from the GHOST who moves closer). The VICTORIAN gets a sink plunger and places it on SCROOGE'S chest. Scrooge holds it and, as the VICTORIAN pushes and pulls, SCROOGE sits up and lies down.**

**The CAST slip away, leaving the GHOST with SCROOGE. The VICTORIAN is last to leave.**

GHOST/FUTURE: So this is how it ends, Scrooge.

SCROOGE: What do you mean…ends?

GHOST/FUTURE: Your stinginess kills you.

SCROOGE: What? I die?

GHOST/FUTURE: Is that what you want?

SCROOGE: No. NO! Please, spirit, take me to the future. I want to see what is to be. Please. PLEASE!

GHOST/FUTURE: As you wish.

**The final SET PIECE takes place. Two bees enter!**

SCROOGE: Oi! When I said I wanted to see what is to be I didn't mean I want to see two bees!

**Two pencils enter (2B pencils of course!)**

Not 2B pencils either. This dream is turning into a nightmare!

**The SET PIECE finally happens – Time Warp to various wrong places; back to the future is muddled with back to the fuchsia etc! It finishes in some disarray!**

GHOST/FUTURE: Sorry. I'm not as experienced as the other spirits! Thanks for trying to take us into the future though.

**The final SET PIECE disperses**

| | |
|---|---|
| SCROOGE: | But what happens to me? |
| GHOST/FUTURE: | That I do know. You survive. You are rich. You survive. |
| SCROOGE: | Well that's all right then! |
| GHOST/FUTURE: | Is it? Take another look. |

**The CAST slowly starts to process through the stage escorted by other CHILDREN with "lighted candles/glow sticks" as quiet music plays. SCROOGE watches. The characters stop/kneel and SCROOGE goes to each one in turn. They do not look at him but leave once they have been addressed. Those not mentioned leave with others.**

| | |
|---|---|
| SCROOGE: | What has happened? |
| GHOST/FUTURE: | Tiny Tim died as his father could not afford the medicine. |
| SCROOGE: | What? But I could have paid for that. |
| GHOST/FUTURE: | But you didn't. |
| SCROOGE: | And what about Bob Cratchit? Did he die? |
| GHOST/FUTURE: | As good as. His family were taken into care after Tim died. He never smiled again. |
| SCROOGE: | Never smiled? Family in care? Why? I could have provided for them. |
| GHOST/FUTURE: | But you didn't. |
| SCROOGE: | And what about that Oliver and the other children? |

| | |
|---|---|
| GHOST/FUTURE: | Those that survived just live rough on the streets. Not enough food or clothing to let them last for long. |
| SCROOGE: | But someone should have helped them. |
| GHOST/FUTURE: | But you didn't. |
| SCROOGE: | How much would have helped these people? |
| GHOST/PAST: | They did not need a vast fortune. |
| SCROOGE: | What do you mean? |
| GHOST/PAST: | If you had given just the cost of one of your precious coffees to charity each day, then the future would not be like this. |
| SCROOGE: | The cost of a coffee? What? Just a pound or so? |
| GHOST/PAST: | Precisely. Just a pound or so. But you didn't. |
| SCROOGE: | And all those people suffered because I was selfish? |
| GHOST/PAST: | They did. Or, to be precise, they will…if you do nothing. |
| SCROOGE: | You mean that I can change things? |
| GHOST/PAST: | We all can! |
| SCROOGE: | Then take me back and let's make a brighter future! |

**By now, all the cast have left but they quickly return to the scene where the VICTORIAN is trying to revive SCROOGE**

SCROOGE **(weakly)**: Cratchit? Bob Cratchit?

BOB CRATCHIT: Yes, Mr Scrooge? Another coffee sir?

SCROOGE: I want you to take my wallet out of my pocket.

BOB CRATCHIT: What? Your wallet?

SCROOGE: **(still weak)** My wallet, Cratchit. I want you to give some money to charity.

BOB CRATCHIT: Charity? Doctor? Has he gone mad?

**SCROOGE suddenly leaps up, shocking everyone. He rushes round giving money to everyone he meets!**

SCROOGE: What a fool I have been! Of course I can spare the cost of a cup of coffee! Why I could spare the cost of a dozen cups… a hundred…. A thousand… a million!

NANCY: A million? Come on!

OLIVER: You couldn't do that alone!

FAGIN: I could form a gang!

DODGER: Consider yourself one of us!

TINY TIM: But how, Mr Scrooge?

LITTLE DORRIT: How can you raise a million by yourself?

SCROOGE: I can't on my own. I just need other people to think the same way as I am going to do!

BOB CRATCHIT: I think I get it! Christmas is a time to think of others.

| | |
|---|---|
| PICKWICK: | We can share what we have with those less fortunate. |
| MRS PICKWICK: | We can be grateful for what we *do* have! |
| TINY TIM: | God bless us one and all! |
| MRS DICKENS: | What a lovely thing to say. I do hope my husband… |
| ALL: | Charles Dickens, the author…..we know! |
| MRS DICKENS: | There! I said he'd be famous! |
| VICTORIAN: | And so will Ebenezer Scrooge. He will be remembered for the day his hard heart softened and he thought of others. |
| SCROOGE: | Can I just say thank you to everyone who has had to put up with me for so long (and I don't just mean the audience!). I am a changed man. Do you know what I feel like? |
| ALL: | Coffee? |
| SCROOGE: | No! Christmas! A merry Christmas to you all! |
| ALL: | And a happy new year! |
| MRS DICKENS (**to husband**): | Mr Dickens! Count us in please! |

**The usual taps are heard on the floor as an introduction, this time, to the final song:**

**"We wish you a merry Christmas" "Thank you very much"
Or other.**

**The show ends…with a collection for charity. Of course!**

Further pantomimes can be found at:
http://richarddecade.wix.com/decade-drama-2014

A Dickens of a Christmas
Aladdin and His Lamp
Ali Baba and the 40 Thieves
Alice in Panto Land
Babes in the Woods
Brian's Got Talent
Cinderella
Dick Whittington and his cat
Jack and the Beanstalk
Joe White and the 7 Dinner Ladies
Peter Pan
Puss in Boots
Sleeping Beauty
Robinson Crusoe
Treasure Island

Printed in Great Britain
by Amazon